CONGRATULATIONS YOU'RE 30

summersdale

CONGRATULATIONS YOU'RE 30

First published as *30 and Proud of It* in 2015

This edition copyright © Summersdale Publishers Ltd, 2016

Summersdale Publishers Ltd
46 West Street
Chichester
West Sussex
PO19 1RP
UK

www.summersdale.com

Printed and bound in the Czech Republic

ISBN: 978-1-84953-901-2

Substantial discounts on bulk quantities of Summersdale books are available to corporations, professional associations and other organisations. For details contact Nicky Douglas by telephone: +44 (0) 1243 756902, fax: +44 (0) 1243 786300 or email: nicky@summersdale.com.

To...

From...

CONTENTS

Thirty? Flirty and dirty!

Anonymous

**Time and tide
wait for no man,
but time always
stands still for a
woman of 30.**

Robert Frost

Thirty was so strange for me. I've really had to come to terms with the fact that I am now a walking and talking adult.

C. S. Lewis

The way I see it, you should live every day like it's your birthday.

Paris Hilton

There was a star danced, and under that was I born.

William Shakespeare

**When you turn 30,
a whole new thing
happens: you see
yourself acting
like your parents.**

Blair Sabol

Thirty-five is a very attractive age; London society is full of women who have of their own free choice remained 35 for years.

Oscar Wilde

Age is just a
number. It's totally
irrelevant unless,
of course, you
happen to be a
bottle of wine.

Joan Collins

Few women admit
their age. Few men
act theirs.

Anonymous

When they tell me I'm too old to do something, I attempt it immediately.

Pablo Picasso

**Men are like
wine. Some turn
to vinegar, but the
best improve
with age.**

C. E. M. Joad

18

Eventually you
will reach a point
when you stop
lying about your
age and start
bragging about it.

Will Rogers

You're not ageing...
You're marinating.

Anonymous

The best birthdays of all are those that haven't arrived yet.

Robert Orben

Let us celebrate the occasion with wine and sweet words.

Plautus

A birthday is just
the first day of
another 365-day
journey around the
sun. Enjoy the trip.

Anonymous

No woman should ever be quite accurate about her age. It looks so calculating.

Oscar Wilde

Every year on your birthday, you get a chance to start new.

Sammy Hagar

JUST WHAT I ALWAYS WANTED

We know we're
getting old when
the only thing
we want for our
birthday is not to
be reminded of it.

Anonymous

Why is birthday cake the only food you can blow on and spit on and everybody rushes to get a piece?

Bobby Kelton

A gift consists not in what is done or given, but in the intention of the giver or doer.

Seneca the Younger

A gift,
with a kind
countenance,
is a double
present.

Thomas Fuller

A true friend remembers your birthday but not your age.

God gave us the
gift of life; it is
up to us to give
ourselves the gift
of living well.

Voltaire

I think, at a
child's birth, if a
mother could ask a
fairy godmother to
endow it with the
most useful gift,
that gift should
be curiosity.

Eleanor Roosevelt

I'm not
materialistic. I
believe in presents
from the heart, like
a drawing that a
child does.

Victoria Beckham

A hug is the perfect
gift: one size fits
all, and nobody
minds if you
exchange it.

Anonymous

Youth is the gift of nature, but age is a work of art.

Garson Kanin

There are 364 days when you might get un-birthday presents... and only one for birthday presents, you know.

Lewis Carroll

Birthdays are nature's way of telling us to eat more cake.

Jo Brand

Our birthdays are feathers in the broad wing of time.

Jean Paul

**The best way
to remember your
wife's birthday is
to forget it once.**

E. Joseph Cossman

Other things may change us, but we start and end with family.

Anthony Brandt

The family is one of nature's masterpieces.

George Santayana

GRIN AND BEAR IT

Getting old is a
fascinating thing.
The older you get,
the older you
want to get.

Keith Richards

I'm kind of comfortable with getting older because it's better than the other option, which is being dead. So I'll take getting older.

A woman never
forgets her age
- once she has
decided what it is.

Stanley Davis

If you carry
your childhood
with you, you never
become older.

Tom Stoppard

There is an anti-
ageing possibility,
but it has to come
from within.

Susan Anton

I think all this
talk about age is
foolish. Every time
I'm one year older,
everyone else is too.

Gloria Swanson

You are never too
old to set another
goal or to dream
a new dream.

C. S. Lewis

No one can avoid ageing, but ageing productively is something else.

Katharine Graham

The only time you
really live fully is from
30 to 60. The young are
slaves to dreams; the
old servants of regrets.
Only the middle-aged
have all their five
senses in the keeping
of their wits.

When it comes to
age we're all in
the same boat, only
some of us have
been aboard a
little longer.

Leo Probst

DO A LITTLE DANCE, MAKE A LITTLE LOVE

You know you're
getting old when
your idea of hot,
flaming desire is a
barbecued steak.

Victoria Fabiano

No one grows
old by living –
only by losing
interest in living.

Marie Ray

If wrinkles must
be written upon our
brows, let them not
be written upon the
heart. The spirit
should never
grow old.

James A. Garfield

The more you praise and celebrate your life, the more there is in life to celebrate.

Oprah Winfrey

Sex in your twenties? 'Yes, yes, yes – again'. Sex in your thirties? 'Ow, my hip'.

Caroline Rhea

The older one grows, the more one likes indecency.

Virginia Woolf

To resist the frigidity
of old age, one must
combine the body, the
mind, and the heart.
And to keep these in
parallel vigour one
must exercise, study,
and love.

Charles Victor de Bonstetten

Do I exercise? Well I once jogged to the ashtray.

Will Self

Early to rise and early to bed makes a man healthy, wealthy and dead.

James Thurber

It's important to
have a twinkle in
your wrinkle.

Anonymous

He has a profound
respect for old age.
Especially when
it's bottled.

Gene Fowler

You know you're
getting old when
the first thing you
do after you're done
eating is look for a
place to lie down.

Louie Anderson

YOUNG AT
HEART

I can still cut
the mustard...
I just need help
opening the jar!

Anonymous

If you obey all the rules, you miss all the fun.

Katharine Hepburn

You know you're
growing old when
the light of your
life is the one in
the fridge.

Hal Roach

I have the body
of an 18-year-old.
I keep it in
the fridge.

Spike Milligan

Bashfulness is an ornament to youth, but a reproach to old age.

Aristotle

Anyone who stops learning is old, whether at 20 or 80. Anyone who keeps learning stays young. The greatest thing in life is to keep your mind young.

Henry Ford

I'm happy to report that my inner child is still ageless.

James Broughton

**Old age is like
an opium dream.
Nothing seems real
except the unreal.**

Oliver Wendell Holmes Sr

**True terror is
to wake up one
morning and
discover that your
high school class is
running the country.**

Kurt Vonnegut

Youth is the time
for adventures of
the body, but age
for the triumphs
of the mind.

Logan Pearsall Smith

Inside every
older person is a
younger person –
wondering what
the hell happened.

Cora Harvey Armstrong

Like many
women my age,
I am 28 years old.

Mary Schmich

Age does not diminish the extreme disappointment of having a scoop of ice cream fall from the cone.

Jim Fiebig

The secret to eternal youth is arrested development.

Alice Roosevelt Longworth

When you're a
young man, Macbeth
is a character part.
When you're older,
it's a straight part.

Laurence Olivier

The ageing process
has you firmly
in its grasp if
you never get the
urge to throw a
snowball.

Doug Larson

OLDER AND WISER?

Everything I know I learned after I was 30.

Georges Clémenceau

You're only as
young as the last
time you changed
your mind.

Timothy Leary

Minds
ripen at very
different ages.

Elizabeth Montagu

You can judge
your age by the
amount of pain you
feel when you come
in contact with a
new idea.

Pearl S. Buck

Age considers; youth ventures.

Rabindranath Tagore

**Ageing seems
to be the only
available way to
live a long life.**

Kitty O'Neill Collins

The first sign of maturity is the discovery that the volume knob also turns to the left.

Jerry M. Wright

Take care of the minutes, and the hours will take care of themselves.

Lord Chesterfield

Age is frequently beautiful, wisdom appearing like an aftermath

Benjamin Disraeli

Knowledge speaks, but wisdom listens.

Jimi Hendrix

No one over 35 is worth meeting who has not something to teach us - something more than we could learn by ourselves, from a book.

Cyril Connolly

We have no simple
problems or easy
decisions after
kindergarten.

William Dean Howells

As one young
man leaves his
twenties behind,
idealism gives way
to practicality.
Almost.

Rabbi Boruch Leff

To know how to grow old is the master work of wisdom, and one of the most difficult chapters in the great art of living.

Henri-Frédéric Amiel

You've heard of the
three ages of man
– youth, age, and
'you are looking
wonderful'.

Francis Spellman

The secret to staying young is to live honestly, eat slowly, and lie about your age.

Lucille Ball

Good judgement comes from experience, and often experience comes from bad judgement.

Rita Mae Brown

We are young
only once; after
that we need some
other excuse.

Anonymous

LIVE,
LOVE
AND LAST

Everyone
is the age of
their heart.

Guatemalan proverb

**If I had my life
to live over again,
I would make the
same mistakes,
only sooner.**

Tallulah Bankhead

He who
laughs, lasts!

Mary Pettibone Poole

Never be afraid to try something new.

Bob Hope

I've finally
reached the age
where my wild oats
have turned into
All-Bran!

Tom Wilson

The follies which
a man regrets most
in his life are those
which he didn't
commit when he had
the opportunity.

Helen Rowland

As we grow older,
we must discipline
ourselves to continue
expanding, broadening,
learning, keeping our
minds active and open.

Clint Eastwood

I'm not ageing.
I just need
re-potting.

Anonymous

If I'm feeling wild, I don't floss before bedtime.

Judith Viorst

The problem with the world is that everyone is a few drinks behind.

Humphrey Bogart

As men get older, the toys get more expensive.

Marvin Davis

Seize the moment. Remember all those women on the *Titanic* who waved off the dessert cart.

Erma Bombeck

You are only young
once, but you can
be immature for
a lifetime.

John P. Grier

The key to
successful ageing
is to pay as little
attention to it
as possible.

Judith Regan

**Everything slows
down with age,
except the time it
takes cake and ice
cream to reach
your hips.**

John Wagner

The best thing about
getting old is that
all those things you
couldn't have when
you were young
you no longer want.

L. S. McCandless

ILLS, PILLS AND TWINGES

My doctor told me
to do something
that puts me out of
breath, so I've taken
up smoking again.

Jo Brand

They say that
age is all in your
mind. The trick is
keeping it from
creeping down into
your body.

Anonymous

**Being a father is
like doing drugs -
you smell bad, get
no sleep and spend
all your money
on them.**

Paul Bettany

Life would be
infinitely happier
if we could only be
born at the age of
80 and gradually
approach 18.

Mark Twain

The older the fiddle, the sweeter the tune.

English proverb

As for me, except for an occasional heart attack, I feel as young as I ever did.

Robert Benchley

Doctors are always telling us that drinking shortens your life. Well I've seen more old drunkards than old doctors.

Edward Phillips

I keep fit. Every
morning I do a
hundred laps of
an Olympic-sized
swimming pool in a
small motor launch.

Peter Cook

Age does not
protect you from
love. But love,
to some extent,
protects you
from age.

Jeanne Moreau

You're not old until
it takes you longer
to rest up than it
does to get tired.

Forrest Clare 'Phog' Allen

I don't do alcohol
anymore – I get the
same effect just
standing up fast.

Anonymous

If you rest,
you rust.

Helen Hayes

Passing the vodka bottle and playing the guitar.

Keith Richards on how he keeps fit

I'd hate to die with a good liver, good kidneys and a good brain. When I die I want everything to be knackered.

Hamish Imlach

CHIN UP, CHEST OUT

After 30, a body
has a mind of
its own.

Bette Midler

You know you're
getting old when you
look at a beautiful
19-year-old girl and
you find yourself
thinking, 'Gee, I
wonder what her
mother looks like'.

Anonymous

I like the idea
of growing old
gracefully and full
of wrinkles... like
Audrey Hepburn.

Natalie Imbruglia

To my eye, women
get sexier around
35. They know
a thing or two,
and knowledge is
always alluring.

Pierce Brosnan

I don't want to
be one of those
middle-aged guys
who turns up with
the baseball hat
on the wrong
way around.

Elvis Costello

You know you're
getting old when
you can pinch
an inch on your
forehead.

John Mendoza

I remember the day
I turned 30... The
way I saw it, I was
never going to age;
I'd just look up one
day and be old.

Terry McMillan

Cheerfulness and
content are great
beautifiers, and are
famous preservers
of youthful looks.

Charles Dickens

Time may be a
great healer,
but it's a lousy
beautician.

Anonymous

Wrinkles are hereditary. Parents get them from their children.

Doris Day

How pleasant is the day when we give up striving to be young or slender.

William James

As you age
naturally, your
family shows more
and more on your
face. If you deny
that, you deny
your heritage.

Frances Conroy

**Alas, after a
certain age every
man is responsible
for his face.**

Albert Camus

One day you look in the mirror and realise the face you are shaving is your father's.

Robert Harris

As we grow old,
the beauty steals
inward.

Ralph Waldo Emerson

**Age is whatever
you think it is. You
are as old as you
think you are.**

Muhammad Ali

If you're interested in finding out more about our books, find us on Facebook at Summersdale Publishers and follow us on Twitter at @Summersdale.

www.summersdale.com